MW01058238

service

Brief Lessons and Inspiring Stories

A book to inspire and celebrate
your achievements.

By Jim Williamson

Edited by Dan Zadra
Designed by Kobi Yamada and Steve Potter
Compendium Inc.

DEDICATION

This book is dedicated to the mentors who guided me; the sales managers who challenged me; the clients who trusted me; the students who followed me; the colleagues who teamed with me; the partners who dreamed with me; and to my wife, Maxine, who believed in me.

ACKNOWLEDGEMENTS

The author and editors sincerely appreciate the following people who contributed invaluable assistance, spirit or content to Lessons Learned: John Becvar, Delores Bergstrom, Dick Beselin, Ron Butler, Tom Black, Steve Cheney, Debbie Cottrell, Ron Crawford, Don Daniels, Curt Dickerson, Cris Dippel, Don Dougherty, Ron Fox, David Haines, Elaine Harwell, Denny Holm, Kelly Holm, Cheryl Hungate, Dick Iversen, Gary Jacobson, Eric Jonson, Harry Mandros, Mark Matteson, Bob Moawad, John Moeller, Anna Nerbovig, Pat O'Day, Vince Pfaff, Dennis Schmahl, Janet Scroggs, Jack Sparacio, Dave Sund, Larry Sund, Ron Tarrant, Greg Tiemann, Lee Tillman, Don Williamson, and Dan Zadra.

WITH SPECIAL THANKS TO

Suzanne Hoonan, President, Advantage Learning, without whose creativity and guidance this book would still be merely a good idea.

CREDITS

Edited by Dan Zadra
Designed by Kobi Yamada and Steve Potter

ISBN: 1-888-387-77-7

TABLE OF CONTENTS

INTRODUCTION

Let me set the stage with one of the most powerful service stories I've ever heard:

Jim Belasco, the best-selling author of "Teaching the Elephant to Dance," decided to follow Dr. Mason Cooley, the famous brain surgeon, on his hospital rounds one week. On the second day, as Cooley was en route to the operating room, Belasco saw the surgeon stop and talk to a janitor who was mopping the hallway. They conversed for nearly 10 minutes before Dr. Cooley finally broke away and dashed into the operating room.

Curious, Belasco walked over and said to the janitor, "That was a long conversation." The man looked up, smiled and replied, "Dr. Cooley talks to me quite often." Belasco then asked, "What do you do at the hospital?" The man replied, "We save lives."

Dr. Cooley's hospital serves as a brilliant reminder that there is no such thing as an unimportant link in the service chain. If you're still working in a company where sales is "your job," then somewhere along the line your customer is bound to hear the dreaded words, "I don't know, it's not *my* job."

The premise of this little book is that the sole purpose of business is to create, serve and satisfy a customer, from beginning to end—and that's *everyone*'s job.

Karl Albrecht ("The Only Thing That Matters") was once asked, "What is more important—sales or service?" He answered, "Neither." He said there is really no point in making sales or service or any other facet of your business a thing unto itself like a strange bump on the organization. The only meaningful objective is Customer Value—the total combination of things and experiences that creates a continuous customer perception of value received.

Delivering extraordinary customer value. Getting the sales and service team to beat with one heart. Focusing on the customer rather than ourselves. This is the spirit of the following pages.

—Jim Williamson

COMPASS POINTS

If you don't know where you're going,
you might wind up someplace else.

—*Yogi Berra*

To ensure that you get the greatest possible value from this book, please take a few quiet minutes to complete the following reflective thinking exercise. A similar exercise is included at the end of the book.

1. My greatest strength in acquiring, developing and retaining customers:

_____

_____

2. One sales situation I'd like to handle better:

_____

3. The person whose sales ability I most admire:

_____

4. The one quality (or qualities) I most admire about him or her:

_____

_____

5. If I get nothing else from this book, I'm going to keep an open mind and look for ways to improve the following:

_____

_____

A BOOK TO
INSPIRE AND CELEBRATE
YOUR ACHIEVEMENTS

OUR MISSION

Service is not just a noun, it's a verb.
It's not just a chart, or a standard, or a
specification—it's a way, a spirit and a mission.
—Don Galer

Great service doesn't happen by accident, it happens on purpose. It's no accident that virtually every company with a soaring reputation for service also has a carefully crafted, customer-focused Mission statement on its wall.

A Mission statement is your company's "reason for being." Typical Mission statements from the 1980's had nothing to do with delivering value to the customer, and everything to do with accumulating profit for the investors. They sounded roughly like this: "Our Mission is to be the sales leader in the Widget industry and to deliver maximum return on investment to our stockholders."

In recent years thousands of excellent organizations have literally stopped to reinvent themselves around the customer. The process starts by breathing new life and new focus into that dusty old company Mission statement. A high-tech company changed its mission from, "Lead the field in sales of state-of-the-art sonar systems" to. . ."Provide our customers with the ultimate in maritime safety and navigation." Can you hear the difference?

Once that company's new Mission—its new reason for being—is up on the wall, every subsequent decision and action by the employees can be calculated to deliver total value to the customer. And an obsession with delivering total value to the customer is the shortcut to delivering maximum return on investment to our stockholders.

LESSONS LEARNED

- *A clear Mission is the foundation for leadership.*
- *Nothing increases sales like a clear sense of Mission.*
- *Is your Mission customer-focused?*

OUR TEAM

Great service starts on the inside of an organization and then works its way out.

—*Bob Moawad*

Out of the blue, I have found myself in situations where a customer service rep suddenly snapped at me. There is never a valid excuse for treating any customer with disrespect, but there are reasons. The number one reason why a service rep treats a customer poorly is because the service rep is being treated poorly by his or her own colleagues or teammates.

Practically speaking, we can't treat our customers on the outside any better than we treat each other on the inside. Great companies know this principle, have *always* known it, and that's one good reason why they last. More than one hundred years ago, Procter and Gamble published a list of Core Values, and it is no surprise to see *Respect for the Individual* (including and especially their own employees) at the top of the list.

The same message goes out from Nordstrom headquarters to every employee: "The better we serve each other, the better we are able to serve our customers." From Einstein Medical Center: "There are no employees here, only internal customers." From AT&T: "Whatever your job, you have co-workers who are your partners, suppliers or customers."

Who are *your* internal customers? How can you serve them better? Do your internal suppliers—your teammates—know what you really need to help you sell or serve? What have you done for your team today?

LESSONS LEARNED:

- *Service is an inside job.*
- *Give and expect the best for your team.*
- *It takes each of us to make a difference for all of us.*

MOMENTS OF TRUTH

One person can *make a difference,
and every person must try.*
—*John F. Kennedy*

Union Bank of California has fewer than 300 branches in the Community Banking Division, but they are winning customers left and right from their bigger competitors. Union Bank does not tout cheaper loans or higher interest than the big guys, but they do lay claim to a very distinctive service personality.

"We call it Moments of Truth," explains Executive Vice President Ron Kendrick, "and here's how it works: Our people realize that we have fewer than 4,000 frontline service people versus five times that many for the bigger banks. But our culture and values give us an edge. We believe that every single contact with the customer, without exception, is a critical Moment of Truth—a golden opportunity to demonstrate to the customer how much we truly care.

"Suppose our 4,000 employees each makes personal contact with 15 customers every day. That's 60,000 Moments of Truth per day, 360,000 per week, or 18 million per year. If you have caring people—and we do—who sincerely believe that every single contact makes a difference, not only for the customer, but for the bank, then you have a unique organization that can compete with anyone in the marketplace, regardless of size."

Kendrick's advice: Convince all frontline people of the truth; namely, there is no such thing as an unimportant employee, or an unimportant task in anyone's in-basket. A great service company is simply the sum total of its parts—so that means everyone must strive to be a great part. Every routine contact with the customer can be, must be, a "Moment of Truth."

LESSONS LEARNED:

- *Every little task in your in-basket contributes directly to the mission.*
- *What you do does make a difference.*
- *Together we can always accomplish what none of us can do alone.*

DISCOVERY

Service is not a list of off-the-shelf solutions, it's a constant process of discovery. To be of real service, one must be willing to constantly discover exactly what the customer wants or needs—and then provide it.

—Mark Ursino, Former Microsoft Director

Great service is never static, it's always dynamic. That's why customer-driven companies such as Marriott, Avis, Alaska Air, etc. churn out so many customer surveys. Tom Pickett of Sun Microsystems puts it this way: "Never try to fit your customers into what you think they want. Ask them, and they will tell you!"

You might assume, for example, that guests at a business hotel truly appreciate a complementary Wall Street Journal—but do they? Marriott's Courtyard took no chances. They surveyed thousands of travelers to pinpoint which amenities should be replaced with others. Maybe a fax machine on each floor is more appreciated than a newspaper at every door.

Not all surveys are created equal, however. In my neighborhood is a legendary grocery store—the West Seattle Admiral Thriftway—that is renowned for its service, selection and creativity. Customers travel from all over to partake in the Admiral Thriftway experience, including amazing samples in every aisle, gourmet cooking classes, and outdoor barbecues featuring smoked salmon by local Native Americans.

Like other grocery stores, the Admiral Thriftway keeps some of those "Tell Us What You Think" survey cards at every counter—but they don't expect to get Native American cookout ideas from those cards. You only get those ideas by knowing your customers intimately, engaging with them constantly, and caring about them incessantly. As the old saying goes, "Get to know your customers, and they will explain your business to you."

LESSONS LEARNED:

- *Survey your customers.*
- *Listen to your customers.*
- *Measure your service outcomes.*

BENCHMARK

Thank God for competition. When your competitors upset your plans or outdo your designs, they open the infinite possibilities of your own work to you.

—Gil Atkinson

Benchmarking is the process of comparing your products, processes or services to the best around—and then emulating or surpassing them. For example, if it takes ten days for you to fill an order, what can you learn from the competitor who does it in three?

And while you're at it, go ahead and benchmark excellent companies in entirely different industries from yours. The airline industry, for example, streamlined some of their customer security techniques by studying the jewelry industry. The fast food and banking industries adapted "drive-in customer service" from the movie industry.

Believe it or not, some companies detest their competitors to the point where they stick their heads in the sand and completely shut them out. But here's a little different take from a handout we use in our seminars:

My competitors do more for me than my friends.

My friends are often too polite to point out my weaknesses, but my competitors go to great expense to tell me all about them.

My competitors are efficient and diligent. They drive me to constantly search for new ways to improve my products and services.

My competitors would take my customers and market share away if they could. This keeps me alert, vigilant and proactive to steadily provide the best service possible.

Each day I thank my competitors. They have been good to me. They sharpen my perceptions and help me grow.

LESSONS LEARNED:

- *Pinpoint what your competitors do better than you.*
- *How are they doing it?*
- *How can you surpass it?*

TAKE TURNS

Caring is your number one competitive edge.
—Tom Peters

At a time when customer satisfaction with airlines has dipped, the image of Southwest Airlines has soared. Who can explain this disparity?

Ron Kuhlman of Robert Roach Consulting theorizes, "Southwest is a well-run, no-frills airline and they always deliver on their promise." Dennis Boyd of the Flight Gazette theorizes: "Southwest is fun, and people like to have fun."

My editor, Dan Zadra, has his own theory, and he says it came straight from Sheila, an amazing Southwest flight attendant. Recently Dan took a Southwest flight from Seattle to Phoenix. He watched in wonder as Sheila moved with boundless energy and grace, successfully calming a crying child, plumping an old man's pillow, trading jokes with the passengers, and answering questions in English, Spanish *and* Japanese.

At one point Sheila spilled an apron-full of pretzels in the aisle and Dan moved instinctively to help her. "That's okay, Dan," she said, "it's my turn."

Impossible! "How do you know my name?" Dan sputtered. "And what do you mean, it's your turn? I haven't done anything yet."

Sheila smiled and answered, "I saw your name when I took your ticket. I always try to remember my passenger's names, it's polite. And taking turns is something I live by. I believe we all take turns serving each other in life. Right now it's my turn to serve you, and I want you to really enjoy yourself on my flight. Someday, you'll have a chance to serve me or my daughter or my Dad. And when it's your turn, I'm sure you'll do a great job."

LESSONS LEARNED:

- *Great service is an art.*
- *We all serve each other, or should.*
- *What goes around comes around.*

LABELS

Consumers are statistics. Customers are people.
—Stanley Marcus

Service is a constant conversation we have with (or about) our customers.

Listen to the talk around your water cooler and you can usually peg the way your organization truly perceives the customer. A study by Leonard Berry concluded that "the language people use when referring to their customers actually signals how they see themselves relating to them."

This is not a little thing, this is a MONSTER problem for entire industries. For example: To the hospital, you're not a discriminating customer, you're a "patient." To the insurance company, you're a "policyholder." To the direct mail company, you're an "entry" or an "address." To the politician, you're a "constituent." To certain salespeople, you're a "prospect." To certain service people, you're a "complaint." And the point is, they often treat you that way, don't they?

I like the way Federal Express perceives their customers. FedEx likes to say that they deliver the most important commerce in the history of the world, and they pretty much treat everyone that way.

If you're a CEO and you need to overnight a $100,000 power point presentation, your package gets royal treatment from FedEx employees. If you are a grandmother and you need to overnight a box of home made cookies to your grandson's high school graduation, are you perceived or treated any differently by FedEx? No, every customer gets the same blue-ribbon treatment, no exceptions, no excuses.

LESSONS LEARNED:

- *How do you really perceive your customer?*
- *Perception is reality.*
- *In public or private, hold the customer high.*

KILLER PHRASES

"No" is a killer word in service. Never say no to a customer; everything is negotiable.
—*Frank Pareta, Xerox*

Just like individuals, entire organizations develop habits of thinking and talking that predict or perpetuate their performance. In fact, I can usually evaluate the service standards in an organization by simply listening to the conversations in the hallway. If those conversations are peppered with comments about "Murphy's Law," then I know that poor customer service is virtually preordained in that company.

Other self-fulfilling word tracks include, "Close enough for government work. . .it's not my job. . .it's not our problem. . .I couldn't help it. . .I didn't think we could do it. . .It's impossible. . . I just assumed, etc."

Disturbing word choices abound in our direct conversations with customers, too. Here is a partial list of killer phrases and their antidotes compiled by Golden Dairies:

Instead of "I don't know," say "I'll find out."

Instead of "You'll have to," say, "Here's how I can help you."

Instead of, "Hang on for a second," say, "Are you able to hold for a minute while I check?"

Instead of, "We can't do that," say, "That's a tough one, but let's see what we can do."

Today, jot down some of the most prevalent word tracks or killer phrases in your organization and decide to turn them around. There is no such thing as the natural law of defects. Let's give Murphy's Law the boot, once and for all.

LESSONS LEARNED:

- *Words are "tools" that trigger pictures and emotions.*
- *Thoughts and words predict and perpetuate performance.*
- *Identify the killer phrases you may be using and turn them into positive words and images.*

BUREAUCRACY

Nothing short-circuits good people and good service like company policy.

—Mary Kay Ash

"Sorry, I can't do that for you—it's against company policy." Ouch! That's one line that is guaranteed to alienate your customer, possibly forever.

Great service is not about customers confronting employees, or employees conforming to company policies. It's about front-line employees empowered to act swiftly and prudently on behalf of the customer. Nordstrom stores achieved legendary service status by empowering employees with a policies and procedures manual that is only seven words long: "Use your good judgment in all situations."

Former AT&T Service Director, Cris Dippel, told me this story of bureaucracy run amok: "When I took over AT&T's Washington Service Center, I was flabbergasted to discover that we would not accept customer orders after 12:00 noon, even in an emergency. Why? Because my predecessor had a standing rule that all orders must be logged and billed the same day they came in. By cutting off all shipments at noon, he could proudly maintain his perfect billing record—but at whose expense?

Clearly we had our eye on the wrong ball. We quickly revised our service to accommodate our customers, instead of our measurement system."

Every company, including yours, has its share of nit-picky rules or policies that hassle and hamstring everyone, especially the customer. I once read of an Oklahoma-based corporation whose employees spearheaded a system-wide effort called the "Gnat Patrol." Its job was to battle company bureaucracy by seeking out and swatting petty annoyances on behalf of their customers. Love that idea!

LESSONS LEARNED:

- *Empower your employees.*
- *Eliminate bureaucracy.*
- *Accommodate your customers.*

SILENCE

Seek out and interrogate your customers.
—Philip B. Crosby

Haven't heard from your customer lately? Don't assume that silence is golden. The average unhappy customer can't wait to tell everyone in the world—except you—about your service.

The Office of Consumer Affairs estimates that only four percent of unhappy customers complain; the other ninety-six percent tell ten others about their misfortune. We have to assume, then, that "No news from the customer may be bad news from the customer."

The solution is to "seek out and interrogate your customers." And when you do, you'll learn a little bit about customer satisfaction from your satisfied customers, but you'll learn even more from your dissatisfied customers.

Subaru of America takes it one step farther. They find out where their new customers did business before and ask, "Why aren't you doing business there now? What made you switch to a new company or a new dealership after all those years?"

The answers help Subaru identify what mistakes to avoid. Another technique, of course, is to survey your fallen-away customers to discover why they left and, more important, how you might win them back.

Moving forward, just remember that there is more good data in a mediocre complaint than in the best compliment.

LESSONS LEARNED:

- *Remind yourself that unhappy customers tell more people about your service than happy customers.*

- *Ask your dissatisfied customers, "What went wrong? What mistakes did we make? How can we win you back?"*

- *Identify what your satisfied customers like most about your service.*

VALUE ADDED

*The difference between ordinary
and extraordinary is just that little extra.*

—Duffy Daugherty

In "Positively Outrageous Service" Scott Gross provides a good example of how easy it can be to add something to your service equation—something small that creates a lasting impression, loyal customers, and terrific word-of-mouth, while costing your company next to nothing:

First-time visitors to a restaurant famed for its desserts are amazed to find a generous and totally unexpected slab of delicious chocolate cake tucked in with their take-home leftovers. As a result, many have become regular customers and have brought in dozens of friends over the years.

I am familiar with a similar restaurant in New York City—one with a Roaring Twenties theme. For years this restaurant has featured an item on its menu that keeps customers talking coast-to-coast, and distinguishes the restaurant from its competitors. Though the average menu entrée costs $35, a huge slice of pie a la mode is only 15 cents (Roaring Twenties prices!) and is delivered with great fanfare to each table.

I have seen similar examples of thoughtful "value added" approaches in virtually every industry. A leading auto repair chain helps customers avoid future problems with their cars by simply providing a written explanation of why something probably broke in the first place. A Kodak copier rep shows customers how to use less paper and toner—even though more paper and toner would increase profits and commissions for Kodak.

The principle is simple and dependable: Often, the surest path to service notoriety is to consistently deliver exactly what you've promised—plus that "little extra something."

LESSONS LEARNED:

- *Put a prize in your Cracker Jacks.*
- *Recognize it is often the little things that become the big things, especially in service.*
- *Look for ways to go above and beyond that which delights your customer.*

SIGNIFICANCE

Everyone leads.
Leadership is action, not position.
—*Donald McGannon*

If you expect to go head-to-head with your best competitors, every person in your company needs to know that he/she plays a significant role on your team. Every employee at Disneyland, including the streetsweeper, is "part of the show." Marriott bellhops are reminded that they are on the "front lines of service excellence." Federal Express drivers are continuously reminded that they deliver "the most important commerce in the history of the world."

To make my point a little better, let me describe just one position on your team. See if you can guess who I'm thinking of here:

Done properly and expertly—the way you need it to be done—this particular job requires discretion, clarity, patience, sincerity, etiquette, high esteem, energy, intelligence, persistence, taste, touch, diplomacy, empathy, communication, public relations, management, mentoring, organization, conflict resolution, a sharp memory, a great personality, high integrity and attention to detail. Last but not least, this particular employee usually makes the first impression—and often leaves the last impression—on more of your customers, partners and vendors than any other employee in your company. Period.

Anyone who can handle all those qualities has to be somebody special. They are. They're your receptionists.

How important are your receptionists? When my friend, Denny Holm, was trained at IBM, their sales training course profiled the average receptionist as one of the "most influential employees in any company."

LESSONS LEARNED:

- *Great service has no role players; everyone's a leader.*
- *Every person in the service chain is vital.*
- *Every job is significant.*

BRIDGES

*Marketing is the process of figuring out
the best way to get all the customers
who are over there, over here.*

—*Dan Zadra*

Imagine a chasm. On one side of the chasm is your company.
On the other side are thousands of potential customers, but
you can't reach them, can't connect with them. What would
you do?

Consider the story, supposedly true, of how they built the
original Niagara suspension bridge. In those days the local
engineers had no way to sling the heavy cables from one side
to the other. So they finally flew a child's kite across the chasm
and let if flutter to the ground on the other side. Attached to
the kite was a string. Attached to the string was a cord.
Attached to the cord was a rope. And attached to the rope was
a cable, strong and true.

Every day I see the sales and service equivalent of the kite
string principle in action. Here's an excellent example, sent to

me by Tom Black, the Executive Director of the Metal Roofing Alliance:

"The metal roofing industry has a general information website for consumers. One of the features is an 'Ask An Expert' section where consumers can ask questions about metal roofing of any type. The Presidents of two of our member companies volunteered to answer the questions on a regular basis, whether they pertained to their products or not. Their motives were good, there were 'no strings attached,' they were simply and sincerely providing a public service.

"But the byproduct of that service was a relationship of trust. Having bridged the gap with the slender thread of email, both men eventually sold many roofs at $20,000-$30,000 each."

LESSONS LEARNED:

- *Become a bridge builder.*
- *Provide a free service for your community.*
- *Expect nothing in return; something good always comes out of it.*

LOOSEN UP

He who laughs, lasts.

—-Mary Pettibone Poole

One year the people at Ben & Jerry's gave this free bumper sticker with every quart of ice cream purchased: *If it's not fun, why do it?* I know a bank officer who was almost fired for displaying that bumper sticker in her office. Her superiors felt their customers might think banking was actually fun and enjoyable—and, gosh, we wouldn't want that.

The truth is, most customers love people who have fun doing their job. If you want riveting proof, read "Fish! Tales" by Stephen C. Lunden. For decades, the hilarious fishmongers featured in that book have worked their magic on visitors to Seattle's historic Pike Place Market. I've been watching them for years and still can't get enough. Their love of life, combined with their sincere passion for their product creates a contagious effect that makes the service experience unforgettably positive for everyone.

More proof: The employees of Southwest Airlines are notorious for cracking jokes over the microphone during takeoffs and landings. Their former CEO, Herb Kelleher, once resolved a lawsuit by bypassing the courts and challenging his adversary to a winner-take-all arm wrestling contest. By the way, Southwest Airlines is currently among the fastest-growing, safest, most profitable and successful airlines. It also boasts the lowest employee turnover and the highest customer satisfaction rates.

One of their company maxims is to "hire people with a sense of humor," and they encourage their people to "adopt a playful attitude. . .be the first to laugh. . .laugh with, not at. . .take work seriously, but not yourself."

Good advice for all of us.

LESSONS LEARNED:

- *Fun is fundamental.*
- *Laughter is the shortest distance between two people.*
- *Enjoy your work, wear it well, and share it with others.*

SPEAK OUT

Mediocrity is the enemy.
—Don Galer

Why do we meekly go through life accepting brush-offs from our cell phone company, car repair shop, or a dozen other service providers? If our own customers deserve the best service, don't we deserve it too?

Personally, I've always given frontline service people the benefit of the doubt. They're human, they make mistakes. But whenever I experience an intentional service gaff, I no longer keep quiet, I speak up—and I urge everyone to do the same.

Recently I waited patiently at a department store cash register while two clerks finished swapping highlights of their weekend dates. I was their customer—barely four feet away—but I was apparently invisible. I didn't raise my voice, but when I finished telling them what I thought about the situation, I successfully raised their service consciousness a notch.

And what about the service that you and your colleagues inside your company provide to each other? If you're going to team up to provide extraordinary service to your customers, you can't accept mediocre handoffs from your colleagues, and they can't accept them from you. Don't let it slide—speak up!

Mediocrity is a depressing place to do business or to live your life. Mediocrity is the place in the middle; it's the best of the worst, or the worst of the best—and who really wants to live or work in a place like that?

Today, think of three constructive ways to begin speaking up about poor service, either on the job, or outside the company.

LESSONS LEARNED:

- *Recognize outstanding customer service and speak out.*
- *Recognize poor customer service and speak out.*
- *If you're not serving the customer, support a teammate who is.*

SMARTER CUSTOMERS

*We can do more than learn,
we can teach.*
—*Suzanne Hoonan*

We learn all about the wonderful features and benefits of our products or services, but we forget to educate our customers. Here's an actual customer complaint that was phoned in to Office Max:

Customer: "I bought a box of computer disks from you on Saturday and none of them work."

Office Max: "Did you format them correctly?"

Customer: "I think so. I even washed them in soap and water, but they still don't work."

Sure, that's an extreme example. But Technical Assistance Research estimates that up to one-third of all customer complaints are caused by customers who simply don't know how to use a perfectly good product. Consumer advocate Bob Filibczac advises: "Either educate your customers, or idiot-proof your products."

Customer education is not just a preventive strategy, it's a proactive relationship builder. Home Depot conducts free in-store workshops for do-it-yourself remodelers. Tools and supplies, of course, can be conveniently purchased in the next aisle.

Imagine legions of smarter customers. What needs to happen after they buy your product, but *before* they misuse or break it? How can you build a lasting bond by becoming their trusted teacher?

LESSONS LEARNED:

- *Go to ground-zero with your products.*
- *Educate your customers.*
- *Teaching creates a bond.*

COMMISERATE

Empathy is two hearts pulling at one load.
—*Dan Zadra*

It's often said that irate customers are the most difficult people to reason with. Not true. The average American customer is both reasonable and forgiving unless, of course, you violate their trust or refuse to hear them out.

Customers don't expect us to deliver the moon, just deliver what we promised. They know our products or services won't always be perfect, but they expect us to stand behind them when they're not—and they also expect us to sincerely commiserate with their inconvenience.

My wife, Maxine, is a flight attendant for Alaska Airlines. Alaska is staffed by well-trained professionals who take quiet pride in their jobs but—guess what?—Alaska isn't perfect. When things go wrong, as they sometimes will, most irate passengers know they can pretty much rely on three things from Maxine or any other Alaska employee: the truth, a remedy, and an ear.

The ear is important. Most air passengers are savvy. They don't expect a ticket agent to repair a grounded plane or to wave a wand and make a snowstorm disappear. But they do expect the agent to be empathetic, honest and as mad as they are at Murphy. Empathy is two hearts pulling at one load, and it really does help lighten the burden for your customer.

One ticket agent who specializes in handling complaints has a dictum she follows: "Take each customer one at a time, one on one, discipline yourself,sincerely commiserate, and tell them the truth."

Then, she jokes, "You go into the back room and scream."

LESSONS LEARNED:

- *Empathy improves with practice.*
- *Give customers a chance to vent.*
- *A problem is an opportunity to show the customer how much you really care.*

IRRITATIONS

*We are all bruised. The motto should be, "Let's
reduce friction to a fraction."*

—Guy Clark

And now a special message for all you small guerrilla
marketers out there. I realize you may not have the budget to
launch a sophisticated customer research program, but down
deep inside you already know what bugs your customers—so
start there!

Frontline people at Lobridge Deli walked in their customer's
shoes for a day and asked themselves, "What irritates me
about our deli?" By the end of the week they had identified
and eliminated 41 annoying items, including brick-hard butter
pats; slow lines in the morning; fruit flies in the dining area; and
thumb impressions on the jelly donuts. Their slogan became,
"Eliminate life's little irritations."

If you still think this advice applies only to smaller companies,
check out this horror story from USA Today: John Barrier, 59,
drove down to Old National Bank one day and cashed a check
for $100. When he asked to have his parking ticket validated,

the teller told him, "Sorry, Mr. Barrier, you have to make a *deposit* to qualify for the parking credit."

Promptly thereafter, Mr. Barrier sent a clear message to ONB by withdrawing $1-million from his $2-million account. Why? Because, like you and me, his life was already too full of little irritations. As the movie character in "Network" put it, "I'm mad as hell, and I'm not going to take it anymore!"

As for Old National Bank, they've since been acquired.

LESSONS LEARNED:

- *What irritates your customers?*
- *Eliminate it. Now.*
- *Make life easy for your customer at every turn.*

SPARE MOMENTS

Make the most and best of your spare moments, and you'll soon discover they become the crown jewels in your day.

—-Ralph Waldo Emerson

As organizations grow, they become more and more pressed for time. They tend to treat people like numbers and confuse services with service. But the great ones fight to keep the personal touch.

For example, how do you end your day? When it's quitting time at Cleveland Xerox, everyone picks up the phone and makes "one last courtesy call." Because it's the end of the day, they don't always make connection, but their 10-second voice mail message will be the first one their client discovers in the morning: "Just thinking about you, Marge, and hoping things are going well. We're here for you when you need us."

When there's a free moment at First Hawaiian Bank, the tellers call longtime depositors to say hello and ask how service might be improved.

Nordstrom salespeople keep their regular customers' birthdays on file, and use their spare moments to send a handwritten card or make a call.

Little things? Maybe so. But, as Tom Peters reminds us, "Perform one 30-second act of exceptional customer courtesy each day. Multiply it by everyone in your organization. Such is the stuff of revolutions."

LESSONS LEARNED:

- *Keep the personal touch alive.*
- *Think it through; team up on it.*
- *A lot can be accomplished in very little time.*

THE POWER OF ONE

Companies, great and small,
Do rise and fall
One customer at a time.
—*Dan Zadra*

"**W**e lost a minor customer, so what? There's plenty more where that came from." Unfortunately that's a fairly common mindset. Many companies still consider sales and service to be a numbers game, rather than a personal pact or bond. They look at an occasional lost customer as an "acceptable mortality."

Other companies, such as AT&T, react to the loss of even a small business customer by immediately sending out their "win-back" team. They are not alone. The QFC grocery chain is one of the most innovative and profitable in their industry. Part of their culture is to impress upon their employees that the loss of a single $100-per-week grocery shopper is not only a blow to company pride, it also represents a cumulative $52,000 loss over the next decade.

Why are some companies so indifferent to losing a customer? I think many American businesses are still conquest-oriented instead of customer-oriented. We want "more" customers when we should be thinking "happier" customers.

If it costs five times as much to develop a new customer as it does to keep an existing one, shouldn't we have more service drives than sales drives? Maybe there's more potential in our client list than in our prospect list.

Ask yourself these questions: How can we keep, serve, delight and leverage our current customers? What are three ways to dramatize the true cost of losing just one of our customers? And what is our version of a successful win-back strategy?

LESSONS LEARNED:

- *Losing a customer is expensive.*
- *Gaining a new customer is even more expensive.*
- *Think "customers for life."*

HEROES AMONG US

In every company there are unsung heroes whose stories deserve to be told.

—*Dave Browne, former CEO, LensCrafters*

Companies that pride themselves on customer service are all different from each other in many ways, but the same in one— they love to tell stories around the corporate campfire.

A good story inspires, educates, motivates and celebrates people quicker than any other type of communication, and has a longer life. Some stories even become legends: The Marriott bellhop who slipped off his dress shoes and lent them to a guest speaker who had forgotten his. The Nordstrom sales clerk who took a Saturday night cab to deliver a new leather coat for his customer's big date. The LensCrafters employees who spend their vacations fitting people in Third World villages with eyeglasses.

Or today's story from a former Lucent VP who told me: "Our lines carry the TV networks' programs, so we authorize our service agents to do whatever it takes to keep that equipment humming. When one of our rookie service people got an emergency call on Sunday, he hired a private plane to fly the critical part to where it was needed. Had he known better, he could have bought a single seat on a domestic flight for a mere $240 versus several thousand dollars for a chartered flight.

"Understandably, his department head was livid and recommended that I write a letter of reprimand. Instead, I formally commended the spirit and courage of his decision."

Who are the unsung heroes in *your* company? When was the last time you told their story?

LESSONS LEARNED:

- *Catch people in the act of extraordinary service.*
- *Treat them like heroes.*
- *Tell their stories, far and wide.*

COMPENSATION

Reward and celebrate
what you want to see more of.
—*Tom Peters*

Years ago a regular shopper at the Neiman-Marcus store in Dallas traded letters with Stanley Marcus, Jr., the General Manager:

Dear Mr. Marcus: I am constantly impressed with the quality of your service personnel. They are always friendly and courteous and treat the customer as king. But I really think you should consider raising their salaries. There is the sweetest old man who has worked in your gift gallery for several years now. His clothes are shoddy and his shoes are worn, but he generally persuades me to buy something. Why don't you divert some of your monies to at least reward your better employees?
— *Lois Anne Baughmont*

Dear Mrs. Baughmont: Thank you for being such a loyal customer. Your thoughts and feelings are most important to us. I want you to know that your letter prompted the Neiman-Marcus executive board to call a special meeting. And, thanks

solely to your solicitude, we voted my father a $25 a month raise.
—*Stanley C. Marcus, V.P. and G.M.*

One of my seminar participants sent that story to me. If you're a star performer in sales or service, and you're thinking about asking for a raise, I thought you'd like it. Or if you are the one who is being asked for the raise, I hope you'll consider it.

Blue ribbon sales and service people are easily one of your company's greatest assets. Honor them. Celebrate them. Reward them.

LESSONS LEARNED:

- *Hire good people.*
- *Respect them, believe in them, pay them fairly.*
- *Get out of their way—they'll knock your socks off.*

LITTLE THINGS

You have it in your power to make someone's day.
—Dan Zadra

It's true. Whether you realize it or not, you and your company have it in your power to make someone's day. And it isn't difficult, and it doesn't take much effort, and it doesn't have to be something big, and it will ultimately make you a service legend, and anyone can do it—so it might as well be you.

I recently stayed with my wife, sister and brother-in-law at the Wigwam, a Starwood Resort in Litchfield Park, Arizona. We had a last-minute reservation and discovered that the resort was booked to capacity. Still, upon checking in, we asked if our rooms could be close together. Darren at the front desk could have easily replied, "I don't think so, we're full."

Instead he said, "Let me work on that, we have a number of checkouts, and I'll try to get two rooms together as quickly as possible. In the meantime, please go to the lounge by the pool, order whatever you like, and the tab is on me."

Did Darren really need to do this? No. Will I always remember my stay at the Wigwam? Yes, because it made my day. Even more important, will I tell all my friends about it? That's exactly what I'm doing here.

Some people refuse to believe that empires are built on thoughtful little details. But remember the Law of Accumulation: "When it comes to making a lasting service impression, the sum total of a lot of little things isn't little."

LESSONS LEARNED:

- *Customer service isn't a big thing.*
- *It's a lot of little things.*
- *Little things really do mean a lot.*

RECIPROCITY

Great service travels in circles.

—William Noyse

The Law of Reciprocity states: "If you do nice things for someone—and with no strings attached—they will naturally want to do nice things for you."

Dave Sund has never even heard of the Law of Reciprocity, but his company definitely models it. Dave runs Sund's Fishing Lodge in Canada. His mantra is, "Serving a customer is my highest calling."

Dave's staff have all made it their calling too. This remote fishing resort has a simple heartfelt training program that would be the envy of any 4-Star hotel. Dave himself teaches the philosophy and practices that make the difference between a legendary "once-in-a-lifetime" fishing trip, and just a fishing trip.

From the moment the float plane lands on the water, Sund's customers are treated like old friends. Employees are trained to have an eye for detail and to look for the customer's needs before he or she even expresses them. Each week the staff votes for the employee who has most delighted a customer. A cash award is presented, and then everyone discusses how to replicate that experience for other customers.

Recently, some California businessmen were headed home after a four-day stay at Sund's. A sudden windstorm threatened to make their flight a bumpy one, so Dave insisted they stay one more day (at his expense) and put his chef to work creating a great meal. The extra day demolished his margins, but that's Dave for you.

A week later, the customer sent a thank you letter, a generous bonus check, and a commitment to bring a bigger group back the following summer. That's the Law of Reciprocity for you.

LESSONS LEARNED:

- *Treat customers as friends and family.*
- *Model and train employees in exemplary service.*
- *What goes around really does come around.*

COMPASS POINTS

We can do more than work, we can grow.
—*Suzanne Hoonan*

1. The 5 most important ideas I gained from this book:

_____

_____

_____

2. Specific techniques, ideas, skills or strategies I will develop and put into practice:

_____

_____

_____

3. If I do nothing else but apply the value received from one lesson, that lesson is:

_____

_____

_____

THE ESSENTIAL DIFFERENCE IN SERVICE IS NOT MACHINES OR THINGS. THE ESSENTIAL DIFFERENCE IS MINDS, HEARTS, SPIRITS AND SOULS

—HERB KELLERMAN,
SOUTHWEST AIRLINES

ABOUT ADVANTAGE LEARNING SERVICES

ALS is a Seattle based training and consulting firm formed to assist companies and their employees in achieving greater levels of performance and effectiveness.

Over the past 20 years ALS has developed and continues to offer seminars in the following areas:
• Leadership • Team Development • Attitude Development • Sales Management • Change Management • Sales • Service • Presentation • Negotiation

ALS has a national account base, many of which participate in their certified train-the-trainer programs. The following is a partial list of our clients:

AT&T	Coca-Cola USA	Weyerhaeuser
Micron	Qwest	I.B.M.
Bank of America	Discover Card	Xerox
Microsoft	U.S. Bank	Lucent
Boeing	Hospital Corp. of	
Nike	America	

Other published products offered by Advantage Learning Services:

"Lessons Learned" Personal Library Series:
I. Sales. II. Service. III. Presentation. IV. Negotiation

Audio/CD/Video/DVD Programs:
• *Increasing Human Effectiveness* • *Team Development*
• *Assessments and Cultural Audits*

LOOKING FOR A KEYNOTE SPEAKER?

Would you like to make these books and other high interest topics come alive at your next sale or service meeting?

ALS provides a number of high interest Keynote Presentations in live multi-media format that will keep your audience's attention, assisting in your meeting's success. Four very popular keynote presentations at this time are:

- *Characteristics of High Performance Salespeople*
- *Gut-Level Leadership*
- *Managing Change in a Competitive Marketplace*
- *Maintaining Winning Attitudes In Turbulent Times*

To discuss availability, contact us at:

Advantage Learning Services
6947 Coal Creek Parkway, Suite 2600
Newcastle, WA 98059-3136

Phone: 425-747-4484
E-mail: advlerarn@worldnet.att.net

Visit us online today and experience our instant Culture Audit at
www.advlearnsys.com

ABOUT THE AUTHOR

Photo Christine Scholz

Jim Williamson is co-founder and CEO of Advantage Learning Services, a private consulting and training organization based in Seattle, Washington.

Prior to founding ALS, Jim served as Sr. Vice-President of Sales & Marketing for Edge Learning Institute, currently an alliance business partner. He also served as District Sales Manager and, later, Director of Marketing for Prentice Hall's Educational Book Division in Englewood Cliffs, New Jersey. Earlier in his professional career he worked as a psychology teacher/guidance counselor at a high school, community college and Washington State prison.

Currently he specializes in the area of helping to develop High Performance Sales & Service Cultures within organizations. He has designed, written and published a number of customized sales and service programs which have been distributed to thousands of employees over the past 20 years.

Do you have a favorite story you'd like to submit? We would like to hear and consider your "lessons learned" for a future edition. Please submit to: advlearn@worldnet.att.net.